Also by Susan Curry

Living On Memory Lane
Visit with Nana and Papa on their lovely country farm.

The Adventures of Little Sister
Join in the wonderful memories of being an active Little Girl

Adventures with the Country Cousins
Join Bud and Sis for a summer of growing up, on a visit to the family farm.

Christmas on Memory Lane
Wonderful memories of Christmas Past on Memory Lane

Off the Page
Fun, fantasy, fairies and a celebration of the seasons

* * * * *

Sing, Color and Praise the Lord (Vol. 1)

Copyright © 2018 Susan Curry
All rights reserved.

In accordance with the U.S. Copyright Act of 1976, the scanning*, uploading, and electronic sharing of any part of this book without the permission of the artist/author constitutes unlawful piracy and theft of the artist/author's intellectual property. If you would like to use material from the book (other than for review purposes), prior written permission must be obtained by contacting the artist/author at:
*an exception is granted for PERSONAL USE ONLY scans and then only so long as any scanned or printed pages are NOT distributed in any manner to any other person, party or parties.

hanfordrose@yahoo.com

Or visit me on Facebook at: www.facebook.com/SueCurryArt

Thank You for your support of the artist/author's rights.

First Edition

ISBN: 9781731065780

BONUS PAGES

'Living On Memory Lane'

'Adventures Of Little Sister'

'Adventures With The Country Cousins'

'Christmas On Memory Lane'

'Be Still and Know' from Sue's book 'Off The Page'

'Praise Him, Praise Him' - New Book in 2019

'Sing, Color and Praise the Lord - Volume 2' - New Book in 2019

Dedicated to colorists everywhere!

IMPORTANT INFORMATION FOR USING THIS BOOK

- This book contains over 36 beautifully hand-drawn illustrations, SINGLE SIDED (back is blank), to color, accompanied by an alphabetical outline of the HISTORY of each Hymn.

- Beside a colorable Title Page and 'This Book Belongs To': Page, there are 27 full size illustrations to accompany each of the histories, as well as 5 BONUS PAGES from the Artist/Author's previous works, PLUS a Preview drawing for the next two books coming in 2019

- The pages are printed on #60 lb bright white paper which performs well for all brands of colored pencils and crayons, without the need of a blotter page.

- To avoid any "Uh Oh's" and the associated disappointment, **Marker and Gel Pen, or any water based media users are STRONGLY ENCOURAGED to USE A BLOTTER SHEET** behind the drawing you are working on to avoid any possibility of bleed through to the next page.

- Most IMPORTANT of all: Relax, have fun, stand-up and stretch often, and remember that sometimes the most beautiful things come from what we think at first are mistakes, but which turn out to be art's way of working magic!

7 BONUS PAGES
from the previous and future works of
Artist Susan Curry

God bless the farmers who feed our world.

© 2016 Susan Curry

'Living On Memory Lane'

'Sunday School Teacher'

'Adventures Of Little Sister'

'The Front Pew'

'Adventures With The Country Cousins'

©2017 Susan Curry

'Angel Choir'

'Christmas On Memory Lane'

'Be Still and Know'

from Sue's book 'Off The Page'

'Praise Him, Praise Him' - New Book in 2019

'Sing, Color and Praise the Lord - Volume 2' - New Book in 2019

History of the Hymns

In this section of 'Sing, Color and Praise the Lord', I have compiled historical information for each of the pages in this book. All of this information is organized in alphabetical order for the names of the hymns.

Amazing Grace – Published in 1779, the words were written by the English poet and Anglican clergyman John Newton from personal experience. He grew up without any particular religious conviction, but his life's path was formed by a variety of strange twists. He was conscripted into the Royal Navy; and after leaving the service, he became involved in the Atlantic slave trade. In 1748, a violent storm battered his vessel so severely that he called out to God for mercy, a moment that marked his spiritual conversion.

He continued his slave trading career until 1754 or 1755 and began studying Christian theology. Once ordained, Newton became curate of church, where he began to write hymns with poet William Cowper. 'Amazing Grace' was written to illustrate a sermon. It debuted in print in 1779 but settled into relative obscurity in England.

However, in the United States, 'Amazing Grace' was used extensively during the Second Great Awakening in the early 1800s. It has been associated with more than 20 melodies; but in 1835, it was joined to a tune named 'New Britain' to which it is most frequently sung today.

Angels Watching Over Me - There is a Negro spiritual with the title 'De angels are watchin' obuh me' which was included in the book St. Helena Island Spirituals. This hymn is often called a lullaby. There have been several versions, the earliest with African-American origins:

'De Angels Are Watchin' obuh Me'

All night, all night
de angels are watchin' obuh me
All night, all night
de angels are watchin' obuh me.

Someday Peter and someday Paul
de Angels are watchin' obuh me-
Ain't but one Gawd made us all
De Angels are watchin' obuh me.-

You git dere befo' I do
de Angels are watchin' obuh me-
Tell all my fr'en's I'm coming too
De angels are watchin' obuh me.

In 1924, St. Helena Island Spirituals published the more well-known, version that sounds like a lullaby.

Blessed Assurance - In 1873, tune composer Phoebe Palmer Knapp played a melody to Fanny Crosby and asked, "What does the melody say to you?" Crosby replied that the tune said, "Blessed assurance, Jesus is mine!" and proceeded to recite the entire first stanza of the now-famous hymn.

Fanny Crosby, blind at the age of six weeks, began composing hymns at age six. An author of more than 8,000 gospel hymn texts, she drew her inspiration from her own faith. Crosby published hymns under several pen names including "Ella Dale," "Mrs. Kate Gringley," and "Miss Viola V. A." Her hymn texts were staples for the music of the most prominent gospel song writers of her day.

Bringing in the Sheaves - The lyrics were written in 1874 by Knowles Shaw, who was inspired by Psalm 126:6, "He that goeth forth and weepeth, bearing precious seed, shall doubtless come again with rejoicing, bringing his sheaves with him." Shaw also wrote music for these words, but they are now usually set to a tune by George Minor, written in 1880.

Shaw died in a train wreck in McKinney, Texas, and a Methodist minister on board said that Shaw saved his life in the wreck. His last words were: "It is a grand thing to rally people to the Cross of Christ."

This hymn speaks to the reaping and sewing taught by Christ, including phrases like "sowing seeds of kindness" and "labor for the Master." Jesus used the illustration of the harvest a number of times to represent the end of the age, a time that should be prepared for by living in anticipation of His return.

Christ the Lord Is Risen Today - This hymn is associated with Easter. Most of the stanzas were written by Charles Wesley, the co-founder of the Methodist Church. The hymn appeared under the title 'Hymn for Easter Day' in 'Hymns and Sacred Poems' by Charles and John Wesley in 1739.

An unknown Methodist hymnal editor later edited it to include the word "Alleluia" to be sung after each line. This results in "Alleluia" appearing twenty-four times in the hymn.

The hymn led to a more popular awareness of Alleluia being used for Easter to celebrate the Resurrection of Jesus. It is an example where Roman Catholics and Anglicans cease using the word "Alleluia" during the period of Lent but restore it into their services on Easter Sunday.

Down To The River To Pray - The earliest known version of the song, titled "The Good Old Way," was published in 'Slave Songs of the United States' in 1867. The song is credited to "Mr. G. H. Allan" of Nashville, Tennessee, who was likely the transcriber rather than the author.

Another version, titled 'Come, Let Us All Go Down', was published in 1880 in The Story of the Jubilee Singers; With Their Songs, a book about the Fisk Jubilee Singers. That version also refers to a valley rather than a river.

Many slave songs contained coded messages for escaping. When the slaves escaped, they would walk in the river because the water would cover their scent from the bounty-hunters' dogs. Similarly, the "starry crown" could refer to navigating their escape by the stars. And "Good Lord, show me the way" could be a prayer for God's guidance to find the escape route, commonly known as 'the Underground Railroad'.

Go Down Moses - This is another African American spiritual. It describes events in the Old Testament of the Bible (Exodus 8:1) "And the LORD spake unto Moses, Go unto Pharaoh, and say unto him, Thus saith the LORD, Let my people go, that they may serve me." This hymn was published by the Jubilee Singers in 1872. The sheet music for 'Oh! Let My People Go' stated that the song originated in Virginia about 1853.

In the song 'Israel' represents the African American slaves while 'Egypt' and 'Pharaoh' represent the slave master. In the context of American slavery, the ancient sense of 'down' converged with the idea of 'down the river' (the Mississippi) where slaves' conditions were notoriously worse. This situation left us with the idiom 'sell [someone] down the river' in present-day English.

Harriet Tubman' was quoted as saying she used "Go Down Moses" as one of two code songs fugitive slaves used to communicate when fleeing Maryland. Tubman began her Underground Railroad work in 1850 and continued until the beginning of the Civil War, so it's possible Tubman's use of the song predates 1853.

Hark The Herald Angels Sing - Charles Wesley's 'Hark the Herald Angels Sing' was published in 1739 as part of his collection entitled 'Hymns and Sacred Poems'. The first line of the hymn originally read, "Hark! How all the welkin rings, Glory to the King of Kings." Welkin is an old English word that means "vault of heaven."

Wesley insisted that his hymn be sung to a slow, somber, and religious tune. It wasn't until the words were paired with a more upbeat melody that it became popular. The current tune for this carol was composed by Mendelssohn, who himself was a Messianic Jew. It is from the second chorus of a cantata he wrote in 1840. Mendelssohn strictly warned that his composition was to only be used in a purely secular manner.

However, in 1856, long after both Wesley and Mendelssohn were dead, Dr. William Cummings ignored both of their wishes and joined the lyrics by Wesley with the music by Mendelssohn for the first time. As a result, the modern version of this beautiful, gospel-centered carol was born and generations have been singing it ever since.

Holy Holy Holy - Reginald Heber was an English bishop, man of letters and hymn-writer. He was a professed admirer of the hymns of John Newton and William Cowper, and was one of the first High Church Anglicans to write his own. In all, he wrote 57, between 1811 and 1821.

Heber wished to publish his hymns in a collection, in which he proposed to include some by other writers. He began preparing the publication,; but was unable to complete arrangements before his departure for India in 1823, where Heber served as the Bishop of Calcutta in October. Arduous duties, a hostile climate and poor health led to his collapse and death after less than three years in India. Heber was only 42.

A collection of his hymns appeared soon after his death. 'Holy, Holy, Holy' was one of those hymns and remains popular after almost 200 years.

How Great Thou Art – This hymn is based on a Swedish traditional melody and a poem written by Carl Boberg in 1885. The author wrote about the inspiration behind his poem: "It was that time of year when everything seemed to be in its richest colouring; the birds were singing in trees and everywhere. It was very warm; a thunderstorm appeared on the horizon and soon there was thunder and lightning. We had to hurry to shelter. But the storm was soon over and the clear sky appeared. When I came home I opened my window toward the sea. There evidently had been a funeral and the bells were playing the tune of 'When eternity's clock calls my saved soul to its Sabbath rest'. That evening, I wrote the song, 'O Store Gud' (O Mighty God)." This song would later be translated into 'How Great Thou Art'."

I Shall Not Be Moved - This is a traditional, African American spiritual describing how the singer "shall not be moved" because of their faith in God.

This song went on to be played by a large range of musicians spanning many genres of music, from folk music, to rock and roll, to gospel/soul, to jazz. It is astounding how such a simple song such as "I/We Shall Not Be Moved," has served purposes from praising God all the way to impacting massive movements such as the American labor movement and the 1960s Civil Rights Movement.

The original lyrics of the song stretch back to the slave era. Typical of many traditional gospel songs and spirituals, "I Shall Not Be Moved" consists of a series of verses wherein a single line changes for each verse. This allows the song to be sung for nearly as long as one wants to sing it, as they can easily exchange a single word or two to facilitate the song's use for multiple situations.

It Is Well With My Soul - The author, Horatio G. Spafford was a devout Christian from Chicago. He had established a very successful legal practice and had invested heavily in real estate along Lake Michigan's shoreline. Spafford's fortune evaporated overnight in the wake of the great Chicago Fire of 1871. In a saga reminiscent of Job, his son died shortly before his financial disaster. But the worst was yet to come.

Desiring a rest for his wife and four daughters as well as wishing to join and assist Dwight L. Moody (a close friend and evangelist) on his crusade in Great Britain, Spafford planned a European trip for his family in 1873. Due to last-minute business matters, he had to remain in Chicago but sent his wife and four daughters on ahead as scheduled on the S.S. Ville du Havre. He planned to follow in a few days.

On November 22 the ship was struck by another vessel, and sank in twelve minutes. Several days later, the survivors arrived in Wales, and Mrs. Spafford cabled her husband, 'Saved alone.' Spafford left immediately to join his wife. This hymn is said to have been penned as he approached the area of the ocean thought to be where the ship carrying his daughters had sunk.

Its somber and peaceful music was written by gospel songwriter Philip Bliss and originally titled Ville du Havre, after the ship that carried Spafford's daughters to their death

Just As I Am - Charlotte Elliott was a Victorian hymn writer and humorous poet. At the age of 32, she suffered from a serious illness that left her disabled for the rest of her life. Although sometimes depressed by her condition, Charlotte always felt renewed by the assurance of salvation, and she responded to her Savior in hymns. She wrote about 150 hymns. Her most famous, "Just as I Am," is widely used in English and North American hymnals today.

In 1834, Charlotte was living with her brother, the local minister. One day when everyone in her family had gone to a church bazaar to raise funds for a charity school, Elliott was left alone, confined by her sickness. Though depressed with feelings of uselessness and loneliness, she recalled the message "Come to Christ just as you are," which she had received from her friend César Malan during the darkest period of her soul. She then overcame her sadness and wrote this hymn.

O Happy Day - Philip Doddridge has been ranked as one of the finer poets of the 18th century. He was a well-respected author, but his best-known literary accomplishments were his approximately 400 hymns, none of which were published during his lifetime. In 1755, his friend Job Orton published 'Doddridge's Hymns, Founded on Various Texts in the Holy Scripture'. 'O Happy Day' is the poet's best known hymn.

Americanization of the hymn took place in 1969, when the Edwin Hawkins Singers' recording of this song was released and became one of the biggest gospel hits of its time.

O How I Love Jesus - Frederick Whitfield was an Anglican Church clergyman. In 1875, he reached the pinnacle of his career when he was appointed to St. Mary's Church in Hastings. He is credited with more than 30 books of religious verse in his lifetime. The first printing of this hymn dates back to 1855.

The chorus is an American melody of unknown origin; but most likely, it came from the camp meeting era. Originally, this traveling refrain was attached and sung with a mother hymn. At some point the refrain of "O How I Love Jesus" was wedded with the verse that begins, "There is a voice I love to hear."

Old Time Religion - 'Gimme Dat Ol' Time Religion' are the first words to this great song that was included in a list of Jubilee songs in 1873. Some scholars who hold that Negro slaves were inferior and incapable creating such hymns would have us believe that this and other African American spirituals had their roots in English folk songs with no historical evidence.

Charles Davis Tillman first heard this song being sung by African-Americans, when he attended a camp meeting in Lexington, South Carolina in 1889. Tillman was largely responsible for publishing the song into the version known to most European-American audiences. The original version of this hymn was also included in 'The Book of American Negro Spirituals' by James and Rosamond Johnson in 1925.

Rock of Ages (Cover & Title Page) – This popular Christian hymn by the Reverend Augustus Toplady was written in 1763 and first published in The Gospel Magazine in 1775.

Traditionally, it is held that Toplady drew his inspiration from an incident in the gorge of Burrington Combe in the Mendip Hills in England. Toplady, a preacher in the nearby village of Blagdon, was travelling along the gorge when he was caught in a storm. Finding shelter in a gap in the gorge, he was struck by the title and scribbled down the initial lyrics.

Softly and Tenderly - In addition to being a composer of secular, patriotic and gospel songs, Will Lamartine Thompson was a music publisher. When his songs were rejected by publishers of his day, he formed his own enterprise, with offices in Chicago and East Liverpool, Ohio.

The words and music for this hymn first appeared in in a collection compiled for Thompson's company in 1880 by singing-school teacher J. Calvin Bushey.

'Softly and Tenderly' is the quintessential invitation hymn in the revival tradition, the invitation to "come home" may also be seen as the invitation to join Jesus in heaven.

Standing in the Need of Prayer – The origins of this African American spiritual are unknown. Both lyrics and tune became well known after their publication in 'The Book of American Negro Spirituals' (1925), compiled by James and Rosamond Johnson. If it were not for the work of these 2 Christian brothers, many of these wonderful songs would have been lost entirely.

Stand up, stand up for Jesus - This hymn was written in 1858 and based upon the dying words of the Rev. Dudley A. Tyng. He preached at the noonday prayer meeting where five thousand men listened to his sermon from the text, 'Go now, ye that are men, and serve the Lord'.

A few days later at his home, he went out to the barn, where a mule was working, harnessed to a machine, shelling corn. When he patted the mule on the head, his sleeve caught in the cogs of the wheel and his arm was horribly torn. A few days later while he was dying, his father asked him, if he had any message for his fellow ministers in the revival. He replied, "Let us all stand up for Jesus."

That message along with the sorrowful news of his death was reported by to the men at the revival. The following Sunday, Dr. George Duffield, Jr. preached a memorial sermon about his late friend, Tyng. Duffield wrote this hymn, based upon Tyng's dying words, as a fitting climax to his sermon.

Sweet Hour of Prayer - William Walford was blind but not helpless or without gifts. He would sit by the fire, whittling out useful objects, such as shoehorns. His mind was active, too. William preached in his rural church from time to time, and composed sermons in his head to deliver on Sundays. He memorized a huge amount of the Bible which he could quote verbatim during his sermons. William also composed lines of verse.

When Thomas Salmon (New Yorker) visited England, he became acquainted with William. While visiting the blind pastor, Thomas discovered that Williams poem/songs had never been put to paper. The men worked together...William speaking the words and Thomas rapidly wrote several of the verses down. Thomas sent the verses to the Observer. 'Sweet Hour of Prayer' was published on September 13, 1845; and a beloved hymn was saved for the future.

Swing Low, Sweet Chariot - This hymn *may* have been written by Wallis Willis, a Choctaw freedman in the old Indian Territory in Oklahoma sometime after 1865. Alexander Reid, a minister at a Choctaw boarding school, heard Willis singing these two songs and transcribed the words and melodies. He sent the music to the Jubilee Singers, and they popularized the songs during a tour of the United States and Europe. The earliest known recording was by the Fisk Jubilee Singers in 1909.

Theories also exist that this song features coded lyrics, ones designed at the time to lead slaves to the Underground Railroad. In this case, "Swing low" is a call for abolitionists to visit the southern United States, where slaves were being held. "Coming for to carry me home." is a plea for release from slavery and a return to family. As for the verse "I looked over Jordan, what do I see?", the Jordan in scripture is the river crossed by the Israelites to reach the Promised Land; but it could be a coded instruction to cross the Red River of the South toward freedom.

The Church in the Valley (Church in the Wildwood) - William S Pitts was on a trip to visit his fiancée, when the stagecoach stopped at Bradford, Iowa in 1857. William had the opportunity to wander through the woodlands outside the small town. He happened upon a particularly beautiful spot in that valley and an image formed in his mind of a church building at the location. When William returned to his home in Wisconsin, he was unable to forget about the image and wrote a poem that he later set to music, saying at its completion, "only then was I at peace with myself".

William Pitts returned to the area with his wife in 1862 he discovered a church being erected in the very spot where William imagined a church would stand. Not only that, the church was being painted brown, the color mentioned in the song.

After the little church closed in 1888, the Society for the Preservation of The Little Brown Church was founded. In the 1890s, evangelists Arthur Chapman and Charles Alexander helped to popularize the song. By 1914, services were again held in the church. As the song grew in popularity during the 1920's and 30's, the church has become a popular tourist spot and remains so today. It attracts thousands of visitors every year to see or be married in the little brown church in the vale.

In the Sweet By and By - Sanford F. Bennett, tells the story of the day in 1868, when this song was born.

"Mr. Joseph Webster, like many musicians, was of an exceeding nervous and sensitive nature, and subject to periods of depression. I found that I could rouse him by giving him a new song on which to work.

He came into my drug store, walked down to the stove, and turned his back on me without speaking. I was at my desk writing. Turning to him I said, "Webster, what is the matter now?" "It's no matter," he replied, "it will be all right by and by." The idea came to me like a flash of sunlight and I replied, "The Sweet By and By! Why would not that make a good hymn?" "Maybe it would," said he indifferently.

Turning to my desk, I penned the words as fast as I could write. I handed the words to Webster. As he read, his eyes kindled, and stepping to the desk, he began writing the notes. Taking his violin, he played the melody and then jotted down the notes of the chorus. It was not over thirty minutes from the time I took my pen to write the words before two friends with Webster and (Bennett) were singing the hymn, The Sweet By and By."

Were You There – The origins of this popular of the African-American spirituals are impossible to trace, borne not from the pen of an individual but out of the communal slave experience. It was first published in 1899 in Old Plantation Songs in the section 'Recent Negro Melodies.'

For slaves, the story of Christ crucified on the cross allowed them to claim Him in a very personal way. Jesus was their Savior who knew their suffering and stood in solidarity with their oppression. In the mystery of God's revelation, Negro slaves believed that just knowing that Jesus went through an experience of suffering in a manner similar to theirs gave them faith that God was with them, even in suffering on lynching trees, just as God was present with Jesus in suffering on the cross.

'Were You There' acknowledged the suffering of Christ, while relating it to the suffering of the African-American community, with its inherent promise of God's presence and resurrection power.

When the Roll Is Called Up Yonder (Sign In Page) – In 1893, James Milton Black wrote the words and music for this hymn which was inspired by the absence of a child in his Sunday school class. When the attendance was taken. He made the comment to his class, "I hoped that she won't miss the roll, when it is called up yonder'. That idea of someone's being not in attendance in heaven haunted Black for the rest of the day.

After visiting the child's home and calling on a doctor to attend her for pneumonia, Milton went home. He could not find one song on a similar topic in his hymn collection; so, he wrote this song. The song's lyrics were first published in a collection titled 'Songs of the Soul', and the song has since been translated into at least 14 languages and sung all over the world.

This page has intentionally been left blank for use as either a blotting page or color testing page.

Don't miss my other books

AVAILABLE in print at AMAZON
(worldwide)
or as a printable PDF download
at MemoryLaneArt on Etsy.com

Made in the USA
San Bernardino, CA
09 November 2019